About this book:

This book is for facilitating fun individual activities or team building activities. It can also be used as art therapy. Colouring images isn't just for children, in France colouring books (art therapy) aimed at adults, outsell cook books!


Page 3: Building - Alter this building to look like another. The individual with the best creation wins. (© amorfati.art )

Page 4: Finance - Caption each of the diagrams, the individual or group with the funniest caption wins. (© Igor Zakowski)

Page 5: Woman Reading: - Alter this image to form characters from a book or tv show. (© ya_mayka)

Page 6: Doodle - Use this page for your own creations or doodles.

Page 7: Laptop - What should be on the screen?
(© gmm2000)

Page 8: Flower - Art Therapy
(© acnaleksy)

Page 9: Caption - Caption this group, what are they saying to each other?
(© NLshop)

Page 10: Doodle - Use this page for your own creations or doodles.

Page 11: Country - How well do you know your countries?
(© airdone)

Page 12: Washing - Caption this drawing.
(© Igor Zakowski )

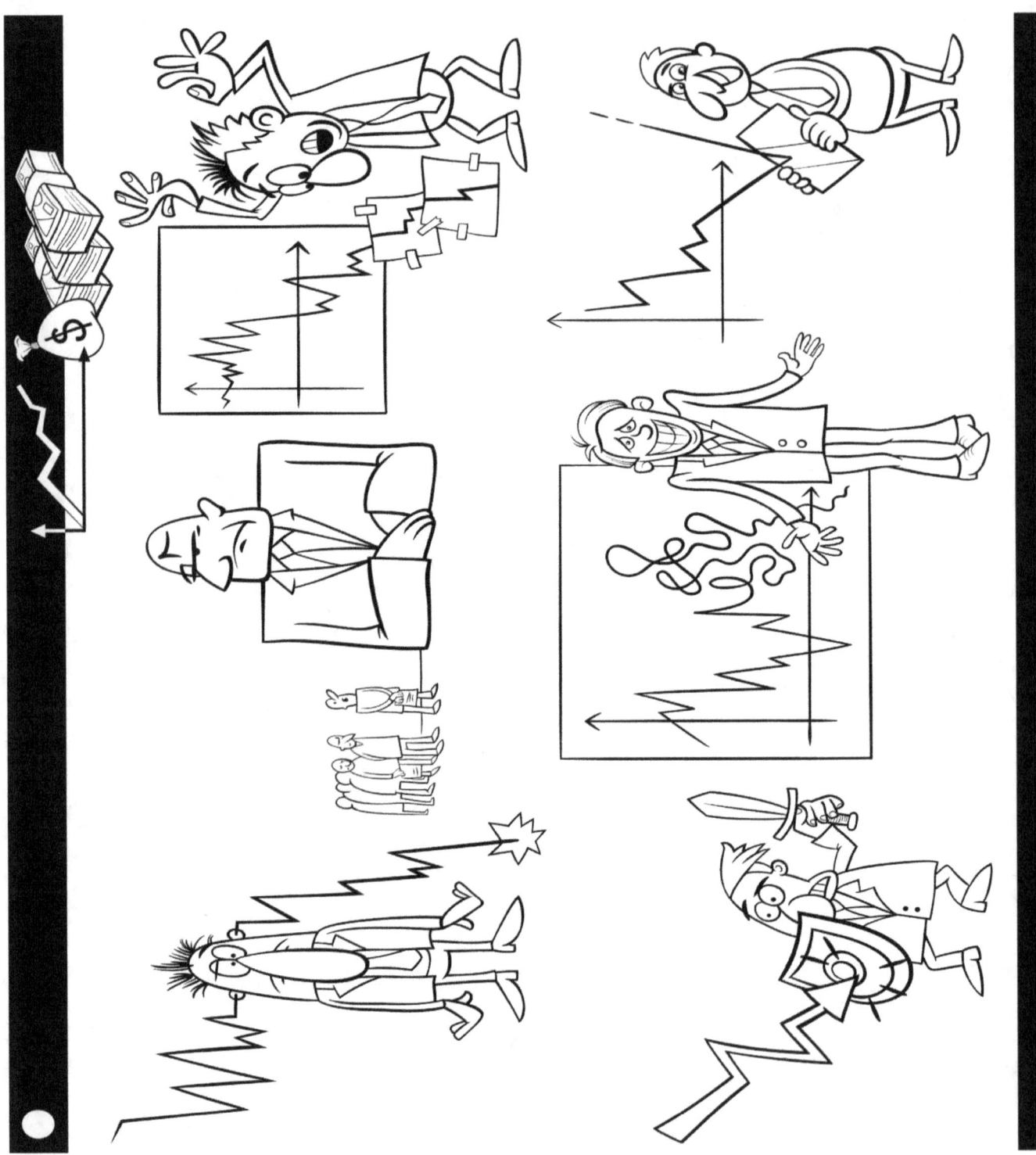

# DOODLE, DESIGN OR TASK

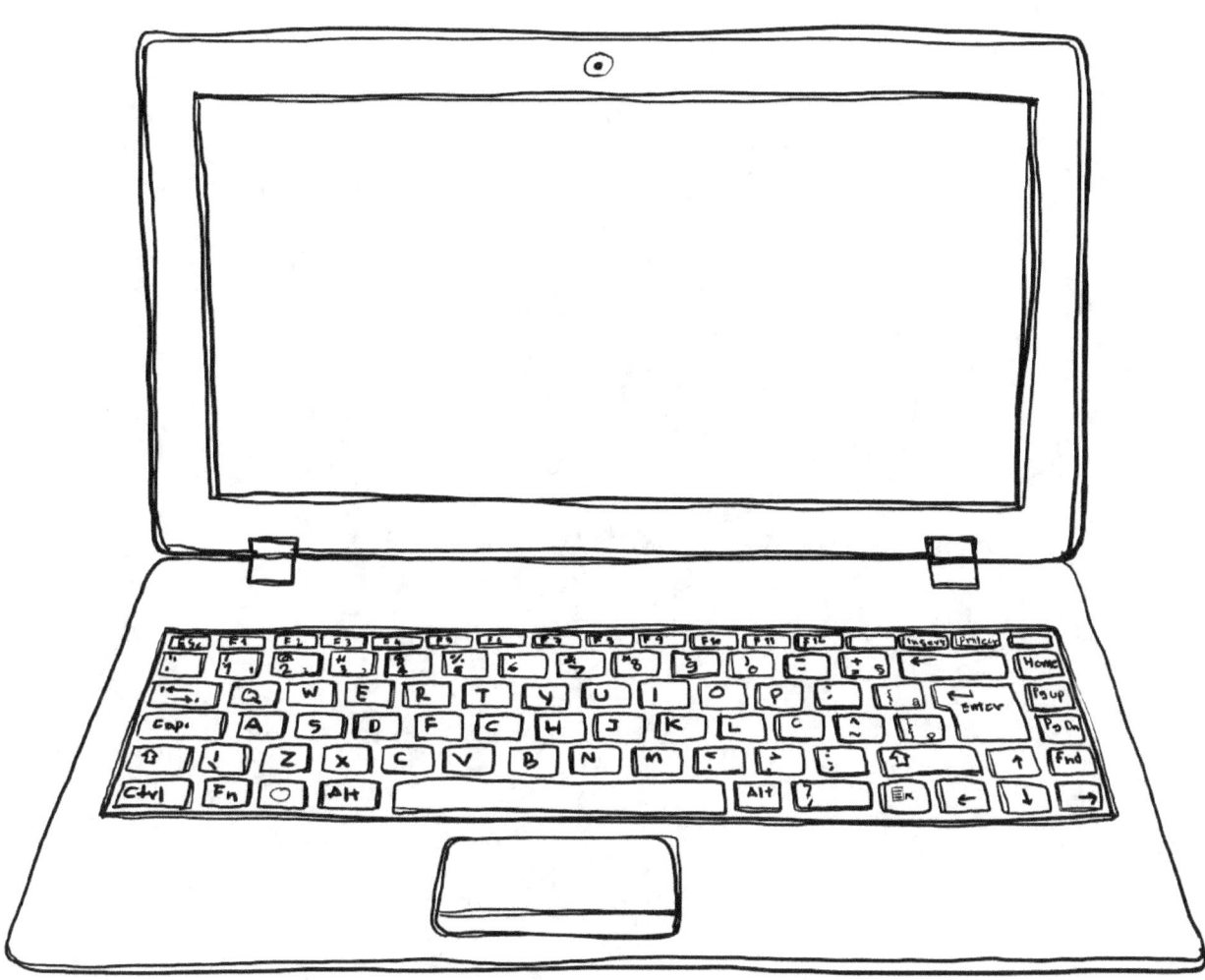

8

# DOODLE, DESIGN OR TASK

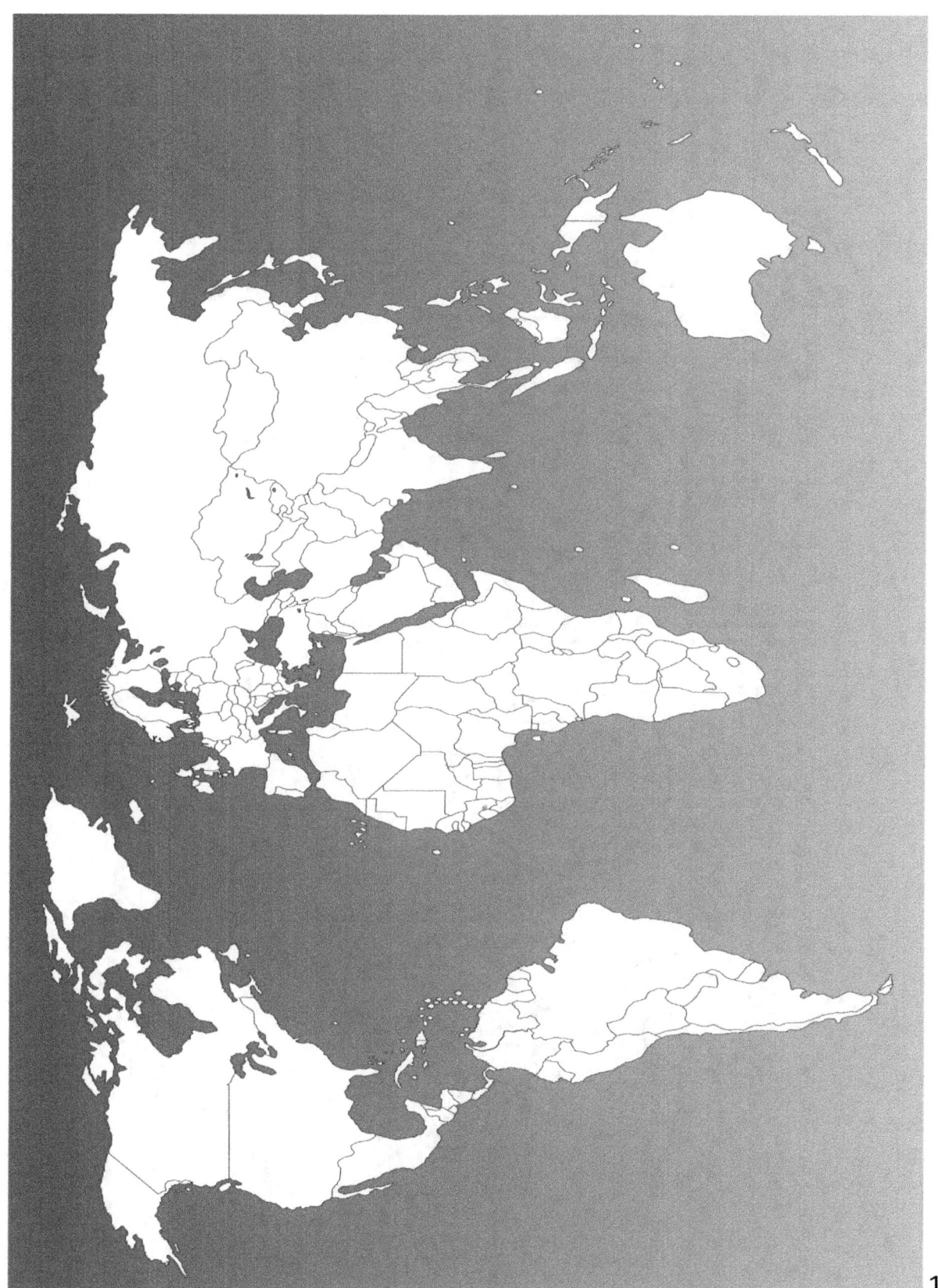

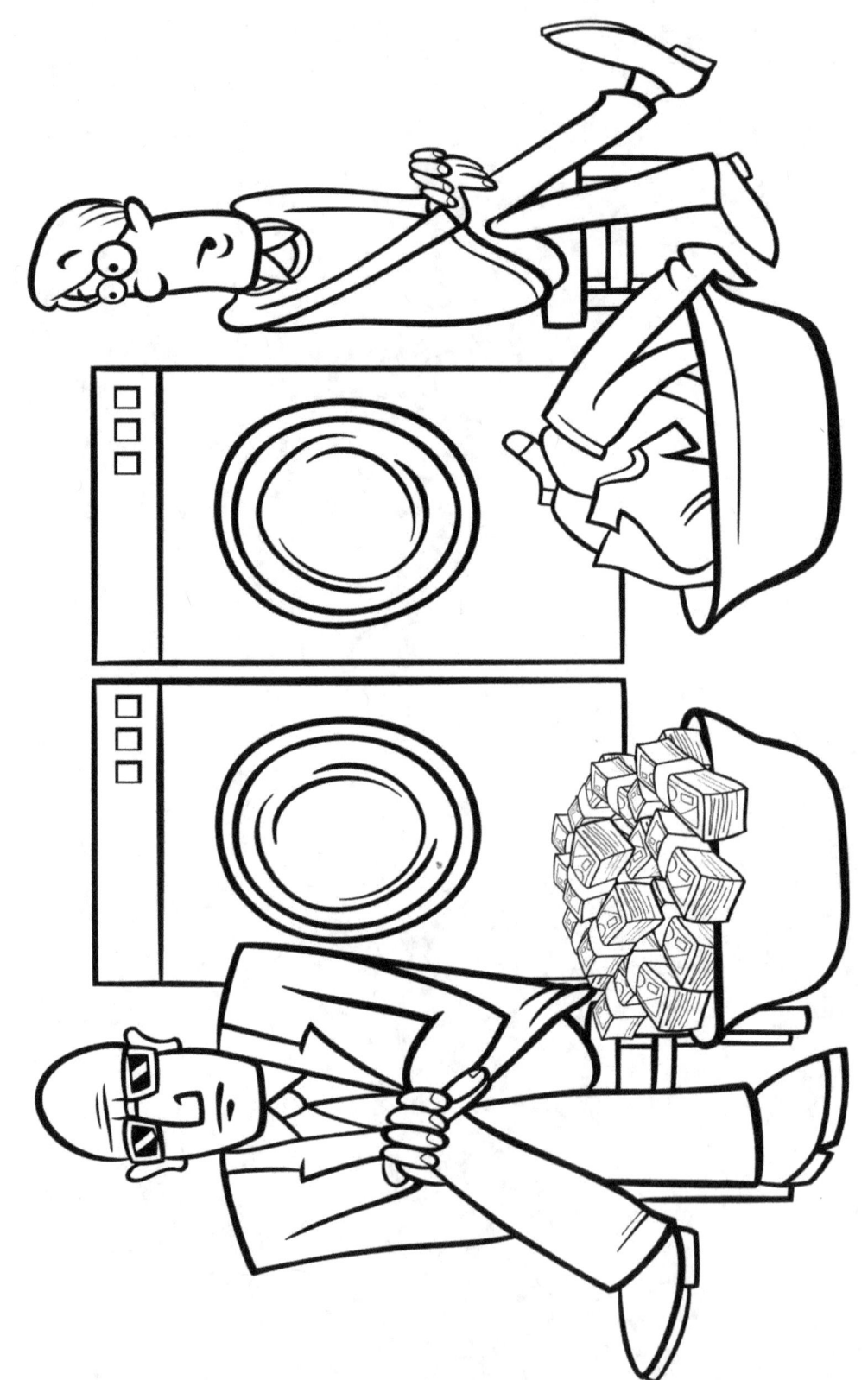

12

# DOODLE, DESIGN OR TASK

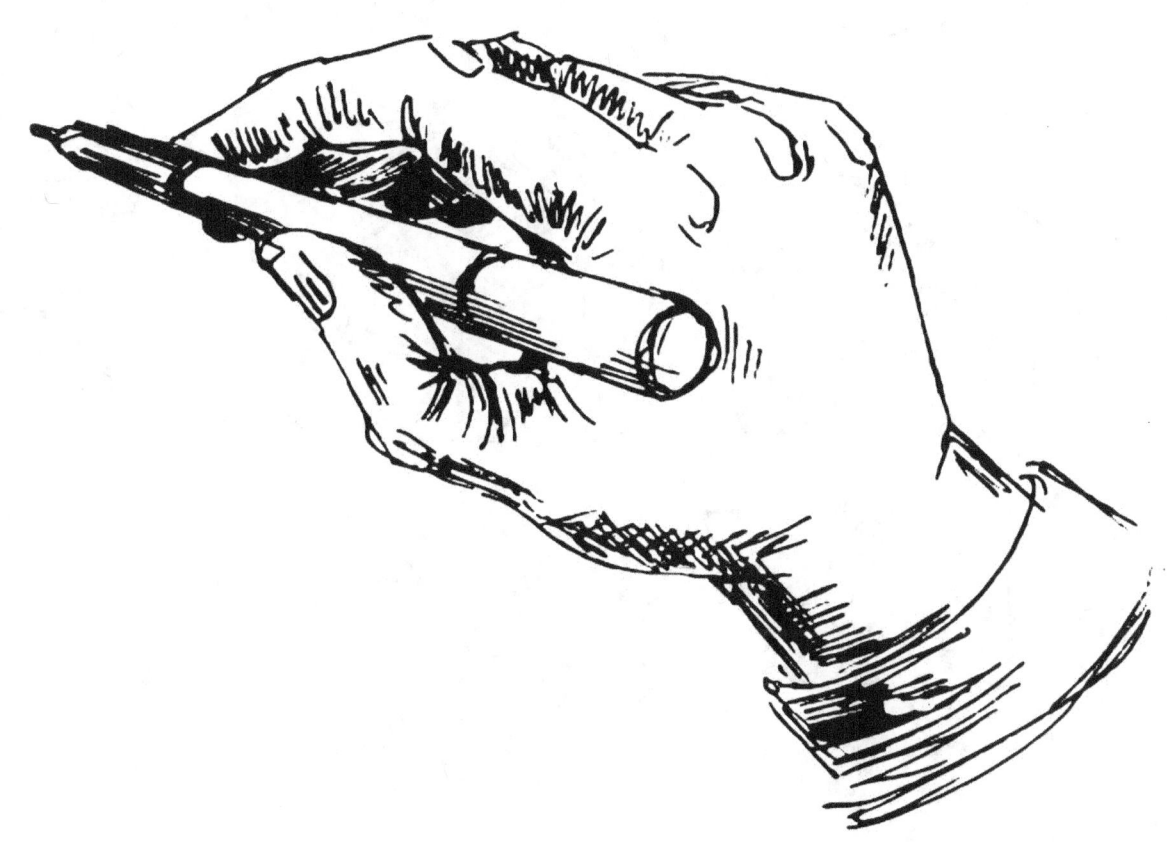

# DOODLE, DESIGN OR TASK

# DOODLE, DESIGN OR TASK

# DOODLE, DESIGN OR TASK